I HAVE SO MANY DREAMS.

Written and Illustrated by Ryan Lim

GRYM BOOKS

Greetings, dear readers!

I am thrilled to embark on this literary adventure with you. I wear the proud titles of a children's book writer and a devoted father to two wonderful sons.
As a parent, I've had the incredible privilege of witnessing the boundless imagination and curiosity that reside within the hearts of my boys. These experiences, filled with laughter, wonder, and the occasional bedtime tale, have inspired me to weave stories that captivate young minds and nurture the magic of childhood.

In this enchanting journey through the pages of my books, I invite you to join me in exploring the wonders of imagination, the power of friendship, and the importance of embracing life's adventures. As a father, I understand the profound impact stories can have on a child's growth and development, and I am dedicated to creating tales that spark joy, foster empathy, and encourage the dreams that make childhood so precious.

So, dear readers, whether you are a parent sharing these tales with your little ones or a young adventurer embarking on this journey alone, I hope my stories find a special place in your hearts. May they inspire, entertain, and become cherished companions in the beautiful tapestry of your family's storytelling tradition.

With warm regards,

Ryan Lim

Hey there, curious kiddos!

Have you ever wondered what you might be when you grow up? There are so many super cool jobs out there just waiting for you to explore.

Let's go on a fun adventure together to learn about different jobs and all the awesome things people do every day.

Are you ready?

Picture this - wearing a white coat and a special tool called a stethoscope around your neck.

Doctors are like real-life superheroes who help people feel better when they're sick.

They listen to your heartbeat, check your temperature, and give you magic medicine to help you feel all better.

Doctors work in hospitals and clinics, making sure everyone is healthy and happy.

DOCTOR

FIREFIGHTER

Imagine a big, shiny red fire truck with sirens blaring! Firefighters are brave heroes who rush to put out fires and rescue people in danger.

They wear special gear, spray water on flames with big hoses, and teach us how to stay safe and prevent fires.

Firefighters are our protectors who keep us safe and sound.

TEACHER

Have you ever had a teacher who made learning fun and exciting? Teachers are like magical guides who help us discover new things every day.

They teach us how to read, write, count, and explore the world around us. Teachers inspire us to dream big and become the best versions of ourselves.

CHEF

Do you love helping in the kitchen and cooking yummy meals with your family? Chefs are kitchen wizards who whip up tasty treats and meals for people to enjoy.

They chop, mix, bake, and create mouthwatering dishes that make our taste buds dance with joy. Chefs use their cooking magic to bring smiles to our faces through delicious food.

POLICE OFFICER

Have you ever seen a police officer helping someone in need or directing traffic?

Police officers are keepers of peace and safety in our neighborhoods.

They wear uniforms and badges, patrol the streets, and make sure everyone follows the rules.

Police officers are our friends and protectors who work hard to keep us safe and sound.

PILOT

Do you love watching airplanes soar through the sky like graceful birds?

Pilots are sky captains who fly planes and take us on amazing adventures around the world.

They navigate through clouds, land safely at airports, and make sure we reach our destinations with big smiles.

Pilots make traveling an exciting journey for all of us.

CAPTAIN

Imagine yourself on a large ship, sailing confidently and skillfully across the vast ocean.

The captain is a maritime wizard who commands the ship through open seas and unpredictable weather conditions.

The captain oversees the crew, navigates the route, and ensures the safety of many people and cargo.

A captain is a leader on the waters, sailing toward the horizon with courage and leadership.

Have you ever looked up at the twinkling stars
and wondered about traveling to outer space?

Astronauts are space adventurers who journey
to the moon, planets, and beyond.
They float in space, conduct cool experiments,
and explore the mysteries of the universe.

Astronauts are like space explorers who inspire
us to reach for the stars.

ASTRONAUT

Do you enjoy painting, drawing, or creating
beautiful things with your hands?
Artists are creative wizards who use colors,
shapes, and textures to express their feelings
and ideas.

They make stunning artworks that inspire us to
see the world in new and magical ways.
Artists fill our lives with beauty and wonder
through their amazing creations.

ARTIST

FARMER

Picture rolling fields of green crops, happy animals grazing, and a farmer working hard under the sun.

Farmers are nature's caretakers who grow delicious fruits, vegetables, and grains for us to eat.

They plant seeds, water plants, and harvest crops to fill our plates with yummy food.

SCIENTIST

Do you love asking questions, doing experiments, and exploring the wonders of science? Scientists are curious minds who seek to understand the mysteries of the world through research and discovery.

They study plants, animals, planets, and everything to unlock the secrets of nature. Scientists inspire us to wonder, learn, and dream of endless possibilities.

DANCER

Do you love moving and grooving to music, letting your body sway and twirl in rhythm?

Dancers are magical movers who express emotions and stories through graceful movements.

They leap, spin, and dance to enchanting tunes, captivating audiences with their dazzling performances.

Dancers bring joy and beauty to the world with their fancy footwork.

Do you love playing instruments, singing songs, or making sweet melodies with your voice?

Musicians are sound magicians who create beautiful music that fills our hearts with joy.

They strum guitars, hit drums, and sing with passion to bring music to life.

Musicians make our world a more harmonious and delightful place with their magical tunes.

MUSICIAN

ATHLETE

Do you enjoy running, jumping, kicking a ball, or playing sports with your friends?

Athletes are sports stars who train hard, compete with passion, and show us the power of teamwork and perseverance.

They sprint on tracks, score goals on fields, and shoot hoops on courts, inspiring us to stay active and healthy.

Athletes teach us that with practice, we can achieve great things.

ARCHITECTS

Imagine wearing a hard hat and using big tools to build amazing things like houses, schools, and playgrounds.

Architects are like construction wizards who create sturdy structures for us to live and play in.

They hammer, saw, and paint to make our world a more colorful and exciting place.

MODEL

Do you enjoy dressing up, posing for photos, and feeling like a star on a runway?
Models are fashion wizards who showcase clothing, accessories, and styles to inspire us with their beauty and confidence.

They walk on catwalks, strike poses for cameras, and embody the latest trends in the fashion world.

Models bring life to clothes and accessories, showing us how to express ourselves through style and grace.

VETERINARIAN

Do you have a furry friend at home that you love and care for? Veterinarians are animal doctors who take care of our pets and make sure they stay healthy and happy.

They examine animals, give them shots, and help them feel better when they're sick. Veterinarians have a special bond with animals and show them love and care.

MOVIE DIRECTOR

Imagine being the captain of a magical movie ship, guiding actors and crew members to create incredible stories that come to life on the big screen.

Movie directors are like storytelling wizards who use cameras, lights, and imagination to transport us to different worlds and emotions. They plan scenes, direct actors, and edit footage to make movies that capture our hearts and spark our imaginations.

Movie directors bring dreams to life through the power of storytelling.

EXPLORER

Do you love going on adventures, discovering new places, and learning about different cultures and environments?

Explorers are brave adventurers who travel to faraway lands, trek through jungles, and uncover hidden treasures.

They seek out unknown territories, study exotic wildlife, and share their discoveries with the world. Explorers inspire us to be curious, bold, and open to new experiences.

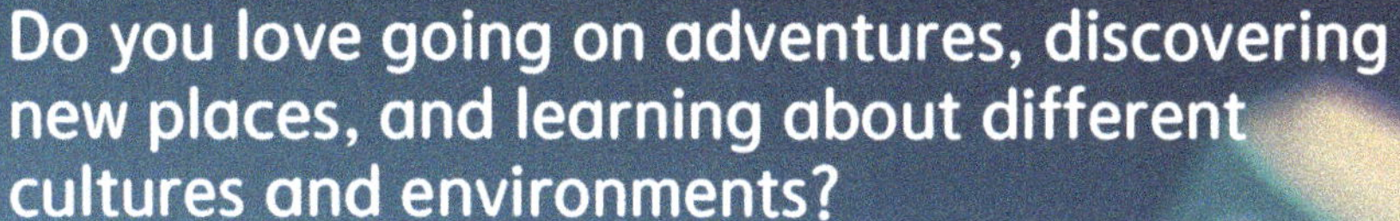

Wow, we've learned about so many amazing jobs that people do every day.

What do you want to be when you grow up?